Mindsongs

MINDSONGS

James L. Harter, Sr.

**Illustrated by
James L. Harter, Sr.,
and David Rodale**

6/3/09
TO SNIP
SING ALONG WITH ME !

James L. Harter
Jim ♥ ER.

VANTAGE PRESS
New York / Los Angeles / Chicago

FIRST EDITION

Copyright © 1988 by James L. Harter, Sr.

Published by Vantage Press, Inc.
516 West 34th Street, New York, New York 10001

Manufactured in the United States of America
ISBN: 0-533-07626-9

Library of Congress Catalog Card No.: 87-90238

To my wife, Shirley, who,
together with my sons,
Jamie, Keith, Andy, and Michael,
gave me encouragement and support.
And to my mother, Ardath,
whose support and love of poetry
made this book possible.

Contents

Illustrations

Preface

I wonder sometimes how the author can write such long and involved novels using great detail, descriptions, and dialogues. He evidently begins with a basic idea and most probably desire, persistence, and then obsession takes over. Usually his vocabulary is exquisite and, in many cases, appears as if he was trying too hard or was proving his intellectuality with his choice of words. In any event, the majority of the reading public accepts the work and perceives to comprehend it.

So it seems to be with the poet as well. I have read and pondered and have been befuddled with more poetry presentations than I have with many novels I have read.

When I write my poetry, it flows swiftly from the pen and I very, very seldom go to a synonym finder or dictionary to seek out that "special word." My poems have been a genuine extemporaneous effort. I do believe that within me the desire and the persistence and the obsession are prevalent; however, there is a haunting feeling that there is a guidance which is helping me to funnel my thoughts into that particular outpouring of words, whether they rhyme or not. I believe that is why the words are simple and become easy to understand, yet the meaning, sometimes, can be profound.

Many people have told me, after reading my poems, that these are thoughts that they think about, but feel that they could never begin to put down on paper. I wonder. I am not that naive or even egocentric enough to believe that I represent them in my poetic endeavors. All I know is that the poetry happens, and I write it down and many times after reading it again and again, I wonder if I was the person who really put those words down. The befuddlement is intriguing, but I will leave it at that and just go on continuing to write poetry the way I have in the past.

This particular collection of my poetry comprises most of the poems I have ever written. Like Chaucer or most everyone else, I too have a closeted collection of bawdy inspirations; however, unlike Chaucer or most everyone else, I was an unpublished unknown. The poetry began originally in high school, and then there was a hiatus for more than two decades when I woke up in the middle of the night and wrote down, in paragraph form, the entire rendition of "The Awakening." All that was changed was the layout of the phrases and the past tense, as it was written, to the present tense. The poetry writing stopped for another sixteen years until sometime in 1985, and then it all began—an onslaught of some sixty-one mindsongs as I like to call them. A word of explanation is necessary for the poem titled "An Ode to the Toad." The poem, together with the artwork, was sent to four couples to attend a dinner to celebrate a yearlong wager that I had won for abstaining from consuming alcoholic beverages of any kind. Except for the poem "A Matter of Timing," which contains the title of the collection and is placed first in the book, all the poems appear in the order of time as I wrote them.

I hope you enjoy reading them as much as I enjoyed writing them.

Acknowledgments

The illustrated artwork in conjunction with the poems "The View," "Shirley's Valentine," and "An Ode to the Toad" were drawn by the author. The remaining seven illustrations, including the jacket artwork, were drawn by my late nephew, David Rodale. The poem "Please Don't Weep for Me" was written and dedicated to David and was read as a eulogy at his memorial service. The poem also appeared in the *Center City News* and was published by his grandmother, Anna Rodale. It also appeared on the invitation for the dedication of the David Rodale Gallery at the Baum School of Art.

"The Awakening" won a fourth place award in a national competition conducted by the Clover Collection of Verse and was published in Volume III by the Petrys in 1970. The poem also appeared in the Jerusalem Lutheran Church newsletter as did the poem "Caring."

"The View" was written when I was at Allentown High School and was selected to appear in the English Department's annual presentation book called *The Canary Digest* in 1950.

Mindsongs

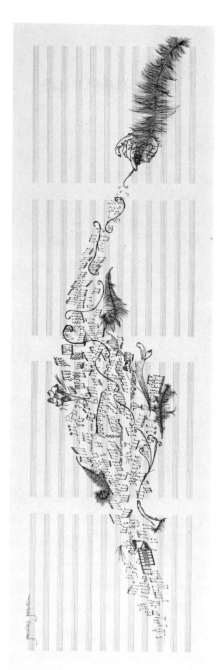

Faeries' Requiem

The Portrait

Jean came to our house
  with paints and palette and brush.
She looked at me and cocked her head
  in a way that made me blush.

The guys were outside playing
  while I had to sit quite still.
But she just kept on painting
  and proved that she had skill.

At last the portrait was finished,
  and the boys came in to see.
And they were all astonished
  because it looked like me.

A Matter of Timing

tick tock
tick tock
tick tock
tick tock
tick tock
tick tock
tick tock
tick tock
tick tock
tick tock
From time to time
        composing the rhyme
                becomes such an easy chore.
But half the time
        lines just don't rhyme
                free verse comes to the fore.
Free verse, you see,
        is something for me
                when I want to merely express.
Since lacking the time
        to compose the rhyme,
                only tho'ts are left to impress.
tick tock
tick tock
tick tock
tick tock
tick tock
tick tock
tick tock
tick tock
tick tock
tick tock
tick tock
tick tock
tick tock
tick tock
tick tock

tick tock
tick tock
tick tock
tick tock
tick tock
tick tock
tick tock
tick tock
tick tock
tick tock
tick tock
tick tock
What comes to mind
      I seem to find,
            is best put down on paper.
If I tend to wait,
      it becomes too late,
            and my tho'ts do quickly taper.
So when it's that time
      for composing that rhyme,
            then soon your mind will discover
That all those things
      your mindsong sings,
            the pen in hand will uncover.
tick tock
tick tock
tick tock
tick tock
tick tock
tick tock
tick tock
tick tock
tick tock
tick tock
tick tock
tick tock
tick tock
tick tock
tick tock

The View

Last year I looked from my window
    and saw a beautiful view,
a view that changed with the seasons,
    a view that was always new.

One day there came some builders
    who worked with bricks of clay,
and now when I look from my window,
    a house is in the way.

Faces

People young and people old,
  people timid, people bold,
  people weak, people strong,
  people right, people wrong;
    all do show upon their faces
    what they think in many places.

One can see upon each face
  thoughts of fear, distress, disgrace,
  worry, hate, and even badness,
  pleasure, hope, and surely gladness.

But tho' these verses seem quite floral,
  nevertheless here is the moral:

    You cannot hide away those thoughts
      that should not leave a single trace.
    Because no matter where you are
      they'll always be there on your face.

Shirley's Valentine

Through any storm or any strife,
my love will climb thru'out my life.
May these two hearts of yours and mine,
abound together in a love divine.
I love you, dear, more than words can say.
This love of mine grows day by day.

The Awakening

The day awakes
    and breaks
    into a dazzling myriad of vivid hues.
Brilliance,
    reflected in droplets,
    clings to every surface.
Thru a shimmering web of silver,
    I see a robin feed and
    a squirrel on haunches munches acorns.
And higher above thru a lacy meadow of green,
    I see the azure blue peeking thru,
    intermittently bringing streams of beams
    to the soft blanket beneath me.

       —and now, right here,—I see Him.

A rippling babbling brook
    intermingles playfully
    among the stately hemlocks.
A trout jumps.
A monarch alights on a buttercup.
And in an eddy,
    the blue and down of the sky,
    reflected on the mirrored surface,
    is pleasantly distorted
    as a water skeeter skitters over.

       —and now, again,—I see Him.

A doe,
    raising her head,
    listens.
And far off
    a dog barks
    and thunder rumbles.
And my wandering mind imagines;
    a baby crying,
    a mother loving,
    a child laughing,
    people living
    In this world,—yet, another world.

                —and, once again,—I see Him.

The day surges on.
Countless little miracles are occurring
    as they did before and will do again.
Now, as those vivid hues
    begin to fade and fuse into a oneness;
    the day makes one magnificent last drive,
    as if it wants to detain departure.
Persimmon sheep
    dance about the orange ball
    and now slowly fade away.

                —and, again,—I see Him.

With the dark comes a new light.
Pins of sparkling brilliance
    sprinkle themselves
    over the dark canvas.
An owl hoots.
A cricket and a nighthawk
    repeat their callings.
A coolness and a freshness
    drift over me.

                —again,—I see Him.

8

My day complete,
　　I close my eyes
　　and everything reflects within me.
There comes a great longing.
My hand, upreaching,
　　grasps a stronger hand,
　　downreaching.
And firmly, but oh so gently,
　　am I lifted
　　into a new
　　and wondrous light.

　　　　—and now, right here,—I see Him.

Ramblings

There was something up ahead which had not given warning,
    or so it seemed.
The feeling of helplessness was overwhelmingly
    draining many desires.
Desires are sporadic and seem to flourish only during
    the emergence of creativity or innovation.
Seems as though the sky and the trees and all that is
    beyond the body is devoid of color.
There appears to be the essence of blindness, yet objects
    have forms not uncommon to the discerning eye.
Drudgeries are shunned with a passion.
Work is no longer fun.
Mind-distasteful tasks are delayed.
Concentration abandons itself to a plethora of fantasies.
The mind leads the body to seek the shelter of these
    fantasies, but the "Mondays" of life inevitably return.
Just like coming off a high.
What leads a being to enter into this euphoria of blah?
Is it a:
        state of frustration provoked by a faltering economy,
            or increasing business complexity?
        Fear of something indiscernible,—shielded by the
            subconscious?
        Self-destructive urge?
        Menopause syndrome?
        Give-up or washed-out stage?
        Lack of direction toward achieving goals,
            or the lack of any goals at all?
        Lack of the inner meaning of life unfulfilled, yet
            understood?
            Or stubborness to accept what is construed to be the
            truth?

Attitude of mind and purpose begins to show its face.
Does laziness emerge as a culprit?
Does laziness deter ambition, or a lack of ambition
      create laziness?
Does ambition require a change?
If the decision is made to make the change, what steps need to
    be plotted to both initiate the change and, if necessary, ease
    the transition?
The being must survive, must cope, must decide, and
      ultimately must solve the problem by himself,
          by himself,
              by himself,
                    by himself, ...??????

An Ode to the Toad

'Tis said:
   " 'Tis loathe to goad."
        But, observe the toad—
        How smug, how cool
        "I'm not a fool.
"I chose the road of the 'Mother Lode.'
Since no booze has flowed, my eyes have glowed.
        Now I squat and wait,
        for that December date
When elations explode and rewards are bestowed
        to the toad! To the Toad!
        For not being a load!!!!!!!"

Just How Do You Write a Poem When There Is Nothing to Write about and When There Is Just No Inspiration, but There Is a Burning Desire to Write Just a Poem?

How do I start,—or worse,
   where do I begin?
I've got no inspiration, darn!—
   much to my chagrin!

Should I think of loving things,
   or could I muse on hate?
I've got no ideas coming,
   so the poem's got to wait.

Oft'times I sit and wonder
   as I dream a rhyme or two:
How can poets write so much?
   What else do poets do?

I suppose their wit and wisdom
   flows swiftly from their pen.
They need not sit and wonder
   how to rhyme this line or when.

Sometimes they take the liberty
   and compose without the rhyme.
I suppose they think this mastery
   is one way to pass the time.

Heavens! Here it is the sixth verse
   and a subject still is missing.
Yet, I've reached my purpose anyhow,
   here's the poem I'd been wishing!

Please Don't Weep for Me

I loved my life and lived it.
There were no "should have beens" or "could bes."
I did what I did, so
                please don't weep for me.

I would grieve
            for the hungry and the homeless,
            for the destitute and the lonely.
I was bountifully blessed, so
                please don't weep for me.

I would grieve
            for the agonies of mankind,
            for the strife, the avarice,
            the prejudice, and the greed.
I am a soul of everlasting peace, so
                please don't weep for me.

I would grieve
            for those oblivious to the miracles
                of the forest and the sea, and
                of the mountains and the universe.
            and for those who wantonly exploit them
                for their own personal gain.
I am of the land and a dweller
  in the house of many wonders, so
                please don't weep for me.

I would plead and grieve
            for those who never discovered
                their talents,
            and for those who did but never used
                them.
I am contented and fulfilled, so
                please don't weep for me.

I lived my life and loved it.
You shared my life and lived it.
We are what we are and always will be, so
please don't weep for me.

I'll Never Understand

I'll never understand the meaning of a butterfly.
    Is it flying butter,
    or a dairy product with a zipper on it?
If they called a butterfly a flutterby,
           then I would understand.

I'll never understand the meaning of a balloon.
    Is it a crazy bouncing sphere,
    or a type of rotund waterfowl?
If they called a balloon a bubbloon,
           then I would understand.

I'll never understand . . .
    A civet must be a diminutive strainer.
    A catastrophe must be a cat with an accent, or is it
        an award for the best cat rear end?
    Is a peephole a throng of persons?
    Cholera certainly is Italian neckwear.
    If a gazette is a miniature gazelle, then can a
        gazelle be a female gazette?
    Is a lisp a slip of the lips?
    An accolade must be an acolyte's helper.
    Is an ant on a wheel called a tyrant?
    Profound must mean a discovered athlete.
    An impasse is the derriere of a little elf.
    And a derriere has to be the aroma around a
        milk company!

I'll never understand.

    Will you?

Thoughts

I am not alone, yet I feel alone;
    for each of us thinks alone.
Some thoughts sure do provoke me.
    There is a longing to seek and a longing to solve.

Why are we here and what do we live for?
Who are we and where are we going?
How do we know the direction and when do we know
    we have arrived?

The life, the love, the soul,
    the understanding, the arrival,
    the before, the now, and the hereafter.

The natural, the unnatural, the unknown,
    the supernatural, the known,
    the earth, the stars, and the universe.

Someone is larger than life.
Someone I know and believe in and someone I love.
So let me be free. Let me fly, let me soar—
    just being free and thinking free;
    non-terrified, non-tethered, non-burdened.

Is there something holding me back?
What is the fear? Or is it fear?
I fear not. Thoughts are raised in the mind and in the soul.
Questions are posed thru the inner feelings and desires.
The discovery is fascinating and a breakthrough is imminent.

Who is the provoker, the seeker, the solver?
Are we one and the same?
The provoker, the seeker, and the solver;
    we are three and we are free—
    but only if we really want to be.

The
Way
Out

Just sitting
and thinking
about entering
into something
                      on the wild side.
I see the road back
as the horizon up ahead
And my appetite is whetted
at the tho't of walking on water.
Looking up at the sky below,
I reach into the depths.
And, disoriented,
find that everything
is merely lacking nothing.

When I stroll
upon the face of the earth
and, inevitably,
face another soul,
I become seemingly aware
and desirous to have
others see me
as I think I want them to see me.

The awareness is,
really,
only within
myself.
And only I,
myself,
can see
the
way
out.

To Aspire to Inspire

What is this stuff about writing something
    only when inspired?
What is the origin of inspirational stuff?
    Is it by the help of God?
    Is it a subconscious or conscious desire?
    Is it an act of revelation?
    Is it an expression or a need to express?

I reach for the pen.
A thought moves from the mind to the fingers
And then from the pen tip to the paper.
And words appear—
    thereafter available to others' eyes.

The others' eyes perform the reverse.
The thoughts are snatched from the paper and
    supplanted into their consciousness.
Meanings or intentions of the author
    might be either transferred or transformed.
Successes or failures of these written thoughts
    depend on how the reader interprets them.

The most interesting aspect of the whole process
    is that an inspired thought usually impacts
    more strongly than those professionally written.

To be a professional writer is a talent.
To be an inspired one is a blessing.

Serenade in Bee

Five Sense Worth

To see, to hear, to smell, to taste, to touch.
Just a little bit of thoughts and such
about those very little things
we don't think about too much.

As I See It

Flirting eyes—cast down—demurring,
    then uplifted—pretense alluring.
Vengeful eyes are pursuing
    those many wrongs of their undoing.
Searching eyes are vainly preaching
    the hopes and dreams beyond their reaching.
Lonely eyes are sadly revering
    elusive friends ne'er appearing.
Loving eyes are befriending
    all those lonely seeking tending.
But of all the eyes, it's those beholding
    the mysteries of life unfolding.

    To see the beauty of a summer storm
        and to watch the flowers form.
    To revel in the changing sky
        and marvel as the clouds go by.
    To watch the bee and ant and bird;
        hurry, scurry, protect the herd.
    To watch the stag in meadow grazing,
        or see the yawning lion lazing.

All these things, and many more,
    freshen my eyes forevermore.

Sounds to Me

The most beautiful sounds I've ever heard
    are likely as common to you as the spoken word.
The fact that remains and startles my mind,
    is that most of this beauty just passes mankind.
Have you ever stopped and listened and really heard:
        The haunting echo calling of a loon
            on a still lake at daybreak?
        The swishing whispers of pine needles
            swaying on a wispy, breezy day?
        The gurgling chuckles of a baby
            gleefully cooing in the crib?
        The crackling snaps of sparking twigs
            in a dancing, entrancing campfire?
        The slurping gurgles of canoe paddles
            as they dip, dip, and glide?
        The first pitter-patter of raindrops
            spattering on the roof above?
        The peace and calm of a normal noisy town
            with all the snow a-lying on the ground?

So next time out—don't shout! But stop and listen.
And you will hear all those sounds that you've been missin'.

Making Scents

The aroma of burning embers in a cozy fireplace,
    or a turkey roasting in a kitchen oven space.
The clean, refreshing ozone smell after a thunderstorm,
    or the essence of a flower bed on a day of summer warm.

The buttercups smell yellow, and the tomatoes smell of red.
    The mint leaves smell green.
But that pie in Grandma's window was the best smell
    that's ever been.
Yet, if this is the time to pick and choose
    and I had my druthers,
I'd pick the smells of that old house
    that once was mine and Mother's.

Palatine Remarks

Not much to be said about one's taste
since sight and smell are interlaced.
One fact remains, we know darn well,
good tastes linger as bellies swell!

Feelings

To see, to hear, to smell, to taste,
    but ah, to touch—to touch.
That's a feeling not to waste,
    and one I need so very much.

Upturned face gathers all the warmth of summer,
    but not too much or next day's a real bummer.
Soft tingling touches caress my skin
    sending goose bumps of pleasure to depths well within.
Cries of agony and yelps of "great pain,"
    when Dad smacked my rear end again and again.

When I discover through the finger,
    the knowledge learned will always linger.
And all the pleasures and all the pain
    will forever in my heart remain.

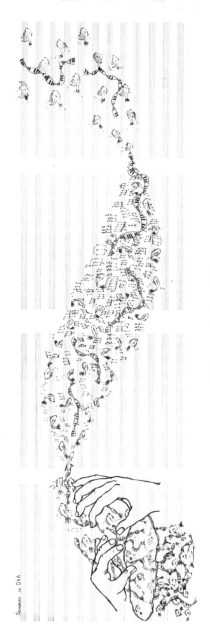

Scherzo in D & A

The Edge

I stand on my edge of this vastness
    as she rolls on in to greet me,
        entwining and tickling my feet.
Each droplet circles and stretches
    until she appears without depth.
I reach to grasp her—
    she recedes to the vastness again—
        returning to unimaginable depths.
Relentlessly, she continues, raging then calming,
    but always rolling, stretching, and receding.
I let this vastness envelop me, and
    I am contented and relaxed.
And I let my body drift as if she, the sea,
    and I were one, and we were free.

    But there remains an awesome respect
        for the wonders and mysteries she protects.
    So I pray for her endurance and safety,
        and for man she oft'times rejects.

I stand on my edge of this vastness
    as she twinkles on in to greet me,
        blinking and enticing mind's eye.
Each star shines and compels
    until the night is a canvas sans depth.
I reach to touch her—
    she recedes to the vastness again—
        returning to unimaginable depths.
Relentlessly, she continues, visible then invisible,
    but always twinkling, enticing, and receding.
I let this vastness envelop me, and
    I am contented and relaxed.
And I let my body soar as if she, the universe,
    and I were one, and we were free.

But there remains an awesome respect
　　for the wonders and mysteries she protects.
So I pray for her endurance and safety,
　　and for man she oft'times rejects.

I stand on my edge of this vastness
　　with the sky and the sea at my feet.
　　　　And with awesome respect,
　　　　stand driven to protect,
　　　　　　the sky, and the sea, so replete.

A Message to Anita

To rhyme the name of Anita,
    use Italian words like *discreeta*
or a local carpet man like Remita;
    but that isn't the proper techneeka.

You're absolutely right, Anita.
    It's tough to rhyme your name.
But if I move the words around,
    I don't have to play your game.

You read my poem the other night,
    and believed it was risqué.
That just seems to show me
    that you don't know how I play.

There are two sides to people,
    as both of us do know.
So when you read my rhymes again,
    please read the lines that show.

For the Home of the Free and the Brave

We are the homeless. We are the brave.
    We are the U.S.A. people that you should help save.
Why the Israelis? Why the Afrikaans?
    Hang in with the U.S.A. and the land for which it stands.

They say this country's great and stands for liberty.
    Can't you help your own rather than across the sea?
They say this country's free and there's great opportunity.
    Why then do we walk the streets while others lap in luxury?

Who do you think you are? Where do you think you'll be?
    If you forget our land—and the people of our country?
The world is watching us and likely chuckling in glee.
    "We'll take your money," they say. "How stupid can anyone
    be?

"Go cut your welfare funds and programs in your schools;
    send money to the world; your destiny's being led by fools.
"Go build your bombs," they say, "to protect your old U.S.A."
    "What will be left to protect if we don't live in a united way?"

We are all Americans, so don't forget my friend,
    we could split apart if we continue this trend.
We are the homeless. We are the brave.
    We are the U.S.A. people that you should help save.

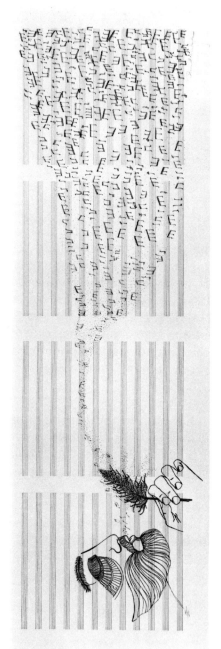

Robert's Dream

Airborne

I am snatched by the wind and whisked away.
I am floating wistfully and wondering
     where the shifting, swirling breezes are carrying me.

I am a dandelion seed.
I am released from my mother, and I am free.
I am free save for the whims of the breezes that direct me.
I am dormant until I gain sustenance in the soil
     and grow tall and fair.
Never to soar again, I await that pleasure
     for the seeds that I now bear.

I am a skydiver.
I am released from the plane, and I am free.
I am able to direct only my descent as I fall free.
I am alive but the breeze and my weight command me
     until I reach the soil and walk,
Only to soar again another day
     if my pleasures are so inclined that way.

I am a hang glider.
I am standing on a cliff edge and am snatched away, and
I am free.
I am in control of my soaring and gliding,
     my rising and descending,
     but the breezes do command me.
   And when I lose the breeze, I return to the soil and walk,
Only to soar again another day
     if my pleasures are so inclined that way.

I am an airplane pilot.
I am starting my engines and I rise to the sky
     under power, defying gravity, and
I am free.
I am able to command the air and may choose where I care to be.

But sooner or later, I must return to the soil and walk,
To fly again, perhaps, another day
        if my pleasures are so inclined that way.

I am a bird on the wing, and
I am free.
I am able to soar and drift and let the winds command me.
I am able to command my own direction and my destiny,
        rising and descending at my pleasure,
        soaring and gliding at my leisure.

        (It must be neat to be a bird,
        or a butterfly, or a bee,
        or anything else in the sky that is free,
        or, at least, seems to be.

        Dreams of being like a bird on the wing,
        to be a flying, soaring, gliding thing;
        dreams like these I seem to find,
        are like realities within my mind.)

I am a spirit.
I am soaring, and
I am free.
        Out of the body and out of the mind;
I am soaring—ethereally!!!

Mother's Eighty-sixth

On this day, May twenty-four,
four score and six my mother reached.
May all the love and moments cherished
continue on and ne'er be breached.

The iris is the flower, the envelope, the bower—
of some brand new poems written.
One poem done this very day—
again the bug has smitten'!

Have a Happy!! Love, Jim

Gestures

I can't quite put my finger on it,
　　but the hand is so intriguing.
Just think of all the simple ways
　　we talk by our hands revealing.

Hands clasp hands and shaking, greeting,
　　gesture simple for two friends meeting.
Palms smack palms like claps of thunder,
　　applauding others in awe or wonder.
Palms grace palms in reverent bearing,
　　releasing bonds of burdens wearing.
Hands together, softly folding,
　　wait in repose to tho'ts withholding.
A reaching hand, a poor soul pleading,
　　"Help me sir, from the life I'm leading."

Arm stretching and hand clenching,
　　anger, envy, rage expressing,
searching knuckles white and taut,
　　for battles fought, yet outcomes naught.
Pats on the back or smacks on the rears;
the former brings friendships, the latter—tears.

The hand upraising, waving madly:
　　"Call on me, Teach, and I'll answer gladly."
"Here I am, I'm so glad you found me!"
　　"Save me please, before the waters drown me!"

The hand upraising, lightly waving,
　　sending thoughts of friendship saving,
like recognition far across the way,
　　or a good-bye sign till another day.

Out of Character

A chameleon sits and slowly changes,
    —color of tree,
        color of leaf—
adapting his skin to many color ranges.

The arctic fox, just suggesting one kind,
    —winter in white,
        summer in brown—
changes his cover and becomes hard to find.

Some types of moths, just like butterflies,
    —mimic an insect,
        blend to treebark—
continue through life in permanent disguise.

An actor, with body, vocal, and facial suggestions,
    —makeup on here,
        change clothes there—
emotes himself up and projects the impressions.

An adaptable person, I might very well be,
    —out of character,
        out of body—
but the person inside me will always be me.

Solitude

At our cabin just the other day,
  I walked alone
and the world was so very far away.

Snuggled there on the northern mountainside
  where the hemlocks, rhododendrons, and laurels do abide;
it is so comforting and easy to blend within
  and let the body find a place to hide therein.

The rhododendron, to be specific,
  sprawls abundantly prolific,
  and, though poisonous,
stands with a craggling, gnarling beauty all its own.

And in blooming splendor, the mountain laurel,
  in its pinky-white floral dress,
punches its way through
  the rhododendron largess.
  (Each blossom cluster holds a separate little flower,
  so I discovered as they dropped to forest floor's bower.)

The hemlocks stand so calm and so serene,
  oases of wonder in so many shades of green.
It's so soft beneath my feet, this needle cushion bed,
  layers of decay waiting for future growth to be fed.

  (I picked up a broken fern and studied and counted
  all the intricate appendages uniformly compounded:
    One of twelve fingers on a branch of twenty-four.
    Two dozen on a limb of again two dozen more.
    Twenty-four limbs and this lacy green array
    contrasts with the brown in this forest floor display.)

Looking down the pathway,
　　many branches frame the view.
Beams of sunlight angle-slash,
　　showing colors bright with golden hue.

Sounds are non-existent, except
　　for a bird's twitter now and then,
and an ever present babbling of the brooklet
　　at the very bottom of the glen.

Nightfall brings the blackest of blacks.
　　Eerie stillness does prevail.
One has trouble soothing self—
　　What lurks behind the darkness, what else does it entail?

I cannot help but wonder, with all the miracles above and under,
　　about the awesome creator of the whole.
Soon a calmness begins brooding, and the mind goes into
　　mooding;
　　I know then—solitude is solace for the soul.

Dreamsport

I woke up in a start this morning,
    and my heart was all a-flutter.
I was looking at an eagle,
    and I couldn't find my putter.   Dreams are crazy.

Standing on the hillside,
    quoting from Lord Byron.
Hastily, I grabbed a twig.
    What happened to my iron?   Dreams are nuts.

Now it came to my turn
    to send the ball a-flying.
But I couldn't get the ball teed up,
    yet still kept right on trying.   Dreams are weird.

I made a perfect shot just now,
    as the ball got lost in sun.
When I strolled to the par three hole,
    I'd made a hole in one.   Dreams are nice.

I place a ball upon a tee,
    and then prepare to smack it.
Tempo, speed, a swing, a miss;
    I don't know if I can hack it.   Golf is crazy.

A little ball, a clumsy stick,
    hit down at it and get it up.
Follow it and hit again,
    until you roll it in a cup.   Golf is nuts.

I hit a ball across the creek,
    the green I had been eyeing.
The wayward shot careened a rock,
    sideways to green went flying.   Golf is weird.

That beautiful shot right over the tree,
    landing softly on the green.
Hand-clapping friends and cries of joy:
    "That's the best shot we've ever seen!"   Golf is nice.

What draws us back to play again?
    How come we love this crazy game?
Dream on, ye faithful golfers;
    each shot brings shame or fame.

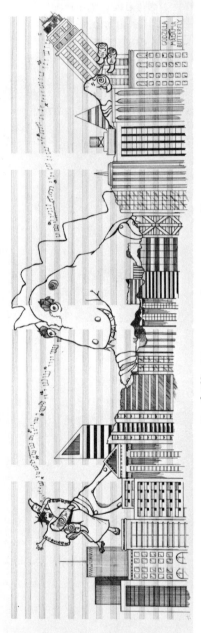

Godzilla Meets Madama Butterfly

Mind over Matter

It matters not what I say here,
　　nor does it really matter what I do here.
What matters most is what I leave here.

Great designs are oft conceived,
　　yet few are ever built.
Men of infinite vision—
　　tho' frustrated, surge on ahead,
　　undaunted, enthusiasm dare not wilt.

Master plans are developed,
　　yet most remain as dreams.
Men of infinite wisdom—
　　hold the keys to constructive progress,
　　but stay reposed in their conservative schemes.

The body of a beautiful woman
　　looks divine in most any cover.
But if she cares or decides to change,
　　one cover merely replaces another.

Yet, the plan of a functional design
　　when clothed in a fashionable dressing,
sets tones and trends of here and now—
　　non-innovating, non-refreshing, just digressing.

A monument to one's ego
　　is not the goal of this man.
Tho' beauty beheld is a factor,
　　the structure's only function
　　is to shelter as functionally as it can.

So it really doesn't matter what I say here,
　　nor does it really matter what I may do here.
What really matters most to me
　　is what I am able to leave here.

Untitled Befuddlement No. 1

Sitting in the barroom amidst the gin and din,
the video is coming off the wall; the mind begins to spin.
Cackling and laughter, jibber-jabber wearing thin.
I don't know why I came here; I don't know where I've been!

The Aliens among Us

I've talked about the mind and how I find
    sometimes
    it's so very easy to write down words that rhyme.
I've talked a lot about freedom
    and being free,
    about being out of the body and flying ethereally.
I know that many times
    ink flows swiftly from the pen
    as if being guided by an unseen force,
    an alien among men.
If I am many persons of tomorrow, then and now;
    what purpose am I in this body
    of which I now endow?
Am I right here, right now learning for a future time,
    another time, another being?
    If that's true, then everything's worth seeing.
There are aliens among us,
    but not aliens at all.
    They are part of all creation and the creator of us all.

On Account of Troubles

Here I sit counting my troubles;
    I'm counting them one by one.
I'm thinking that all of my troubles
    are creating a life without fun.

But then, thinking of all of the troubles
    that the rest of the world is in;
I sit here grinning away my troubles,
    counting those I'm not included in.

Are you thinking that all of your troubles
    are awful and should not ever be?
Please, when you are counting your troubles,
    just grin, and write poetry.
                Like me!!

Chairman of the Bored

Just bored,
        (not life bored),
        just bored.
What to do?
Pick up walnuts? Clean windows? Weed?
                                          Blah!!!

Beautiful day.
Just sit
        here in this chair.
Nice,
        but boring.
Golfed today. Played lousy.
Should have stayed home on this chair.
And done what?
              Nothing.
                    Boring!!
Ended up picking up walnuts.
                                          Blah!!!

What to do now?
Just sit
        here in this chair.
Want a beer?
              Thanks, don't mind if I do.
Relax!
        In this chair relaxed.
                    Boring!!
But who cares now?
I am here in this chair, relaxed, and
        the beer tastes oh so good!
                                      Ah!!!!!!!!

Untitled Befuddlement No. 2

Logic is sensible; nonsense is not.
If sensible nonsense is logical—then what?

Untitled Befuddlement No. 3

I can stand and point and gaze on upward.
  Others wonder and point and look up, too.
  I could leave and all those pointers
  would continue gazing and so would you.

Untitled Befuddlement No. 4

"If I am your shepherd and you are my sheep,
    as I watch and protect you, so calmly you keep.
Should my staff and my presence forthwith disappear;
    Tho' you are many and mighty, you'd cower in fear."

The strong ones emerge to the edge of the circle.
Still fearful, but commanding, urge followers to encircle.

Each group takes to their own ways, traversing the land,
expanding their flocks and taking their stand.

Fear is disguised by their faith in those preaching,
demigods whose power and greed keep right on reaching.

War and pestilence prevail, and fear keeps increasing.
Until, through a deafening crescendo, there's peace—
                 all else ceasing.

The flocks have regrouped and are calmly returning,
awaiting the appearance of the shepherd they're yearning.

"If I am your shepherd and you are my sheep,
    as I watch and protect you, so calmly you keep.
Should my staff and my presence forthwith disappear;
    tho' you are many and mighty, you'd cower in fear.

"How many times must I stand here before you?
    How many times must I comfort and console you?
When will you learn to love all I begat?
    When will my absence be just nothing but that?
What do you fear and why do you fear it?
    I am always right near you; don't doubt,
                 just believe it!!"

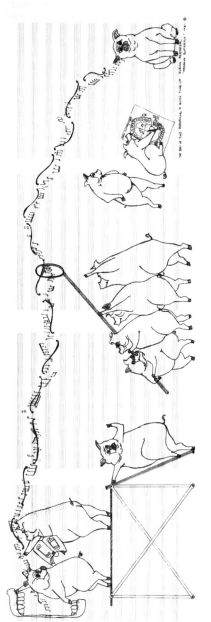

The Bay of Pigs

Highpoints   (Befuddlement No. 3 Revisited)

I can stand and point on upward.
    Others wonder and point and look up, too.
I could leave and all those pointers
    would continue right on gazing.
        Would those gazers include you?

Is there something to be learned here
    as one's imagination runs amok?
I think I could create a false belief
    with a touch of persuasion
        and just a little bit of luck.

How many pointers walk across these lands?
    How many followers lift up their hands?
These salesmen of faith keep reaping all the profits
    while the blind buyers of hope
        dig deeper into their pockets.

So take heed, all of you pointers;
    some day we'll see the light.
We'll stand up tall and walk away,
    discovering which way is right.
And all those hopeless pointers
    still thinking they're men of might
will preach and plead through their own greed,
    until they fade on into the night.

Owl Tell

High in his tree sat the sage old bard owl,
    staring me down with eyes dark as earth's bowel.
Thoughts lurk in those depths, I suddenly pondered.
    If I speak unto him, will he answer? I wondered.
From out of my pocket, I offered a treat,
    which he readily accepted, then returned to his seat.
There again did he sit, so high in his tree,
    and again that blank stare looked down upon me.
I fitfully blundered and stammered and stuttered,
    but soon, with composure, I finally muttered:
"I am but a poor man out walking this land.
    Would you, kind sir, please give me a hand?
Befuddled and frustrated I do seem to be.
    Would you answer these questions bothering me?
What songs will you sing me? What words can you offer?
    Is there rhyme or reason in your unfathomable coffer?
Teach me the ways or show me the right path
    that man needs to take to ward off life's wrath.
I look up to you, 'Bard', so high in the sky.
    I've got to believe you're more'n meets the eye."

"I'll tell you," quipped he with a blink of an eye,
    "walk strongly, stand proudly, and never say die.
Believe in yourself; be happy, be free,
    be kind to all others, just as you are with me.
Help whom you can and how quickly you'll see;
    that life is worth living and death ne'er will be."

"Thank you," I said to the owl in his tree.
    "I know now what I should, and my mind is set free.
Yes, I know what I am and am happy to be
    a friend to all things above and under the sea.
I'll remember your wisdom and the lines you have sung;
    and I'll tell unto others every word, O Great One!"

Quintessence: Reflections

If I am on the outside looking in,
        and you are on the inside looking out,
when our gazes finally meet,
        will we know then what life is all about?

I am looking unto myself,
        and I see myself as I was.
But "what I was" is unclear
        to me as what I am.

I am looking unto myself,
        and I see myself as I am.
But still, it is unclear to me
        that I really am what I am.

I am looking unto myself,
        and I see myself as I might be.
And again, it is still unclear to me
        that what I see is what I am to be.

If "what I am" and "what I was" are part of just
        a learning tree for what I am to be;
then what I do when "what I am"
        will lead me on to be what I am to be.

Quintessence: Scenario

The day starts slow
    and doesn't pick up
until
    the sun meets the other side of the sky.
The night winds blow,
    and suddenly,
I am picked up and carried
    into the depths of the night.
Yet there is no night.
There is a light—
    a light so bright
that I reach with all my might
    and touch the light.
And suddenly, all my dreams
    are consummated in those bright beams.
And I am blessed with becoming part of all those scenes
    in all those dreams.
Bright Light.
        Life Bright.
             Life Light.
                I am turned on . . .

Quintessence: Breakthrough

I am ecstatic.
I have found something beyond belief.
      Well, not beyond belief to me,
      but perhaps to those eyes that
      read between these lines.
I have a feeling of reaching a plateau—
      a plateau of understanding,
      comprehending, and condescending.
I am ready to move on. Yet moving on
      needs more seeking and searching,
      more reaching and learning.
I am ready.
I will move on.
I will become.
I will be . . .

Quintessence: Perspective

Let's step back a minute
>and panoramically study the whole scene.

Let's peruse
>what has happened here and what you mean

To me: You are the Master Controller
>of my life and being.
>You are my walking, talking,
>>sleeping, seeing.

To me: You are the Creator
>of all that is living and all that is not.
>You are every star, every raindrop,
>>and everything at every spot.

To me: You are the Direction of my destiny and my life.
>You are my leading, guiding, and encouraging.
>You are the Breakthrough,
>>the Cutting Edge to renewed life.

To me: You are the Answer
>to my seeking, searching, reaching, learning.
>You are the Direction for which I've been yearning.

To me: You are the Ultimate,
>the Rapture, the Ecstacy, the Light.
>You are the Omnipresence,
>>the Soaring Spirit that ne'er is out of sight.

Quintessence: Why Me?

But yet, there remains this haunting feeling of "why me?"
    So insignificant,
        like a single drop of rain, or
        from a massive forest, a single leaf
        from a teeny tiny tree.
Yet each and every single drop of falling rain,
        and each and every leaf upon that little tree
becomes a part of His whole scheme.
        And therein lies the everlasting dream.

I am part of Him, and He is part of me.
And somehow, someday, someway;
        we will all together be.

Moving Thoughts

Seeing, reaching, seeking, breeching, mind expanding,
      moving on.
Life light burning, love light yearning, songs of mind,
      singing strong.
Mind enhancing, thoughts entrancing, meditation,
      coming on.
Floating, drifting, spirit lifting, silver thread,
      holding on.
Light adoring, spirit soaring, breaking tether,
      ascending on.
Life light reaching, love beseeching, I am learning,
      and moving on . . .

I Am What I Am

I am.

He is.

We are.   Inside me is He.
And we are one being.

Being

what we are

we are what we believe in.

Believing in

what we are is what we will be.

What we believe we will be is one being.

He is
inside me
and I am Him.
Therefore, I am.

I am a universe unto myself.

I am the co-creator.

The God I am is within me.

If I am God

then I
and He
are within me.

And we are one.

When I talk to God,
I am talking to myself,
and his answers are within me.

But wherefore the tether and why the release?

The tether is the bond between
the ethereal and physical planes.

The release is the reaching of the plateau
of knowledge and understanding, and
the acceptance and willingness to continue
learning at a higher plane.
I am what I am
and His presence is within me.
Understanding and accepting is now up to me.

Days of Yore

Something big was really comin' down,
up along the Lehigh in ole' Laurytown.
'Twas 'bout eighteen hundred and thirty-seven—
all hell broke loose in that forested heaven.
Trees a-tumblin' started the sawmills a-buzzin',
a-buildin' that canal and barges by the dozen.
No one even dreamed buildin' the canal would be silly.
In no time at all, the feat went right on down to Philly!
Every Sunday, that town at the base of wooded glen
filled to the hilt with a thousand thirsty men.
Yep! Take any bright and sunny summer Sunday afternoon;
it's going down at ole' Jake Morris's log cabin saloon.
See men a-standin', screamin', drinkin' whiskey oh so fine,
buckets bein' passed on down to those a-waitin' in the line.
Tin cups all a-flyin' and into buckets swiftly dippin';
Nary a man was there who was ever caught just sippin'.

There they all were, playin' cards and shootin' mark,
a-fightin' and a-carousin' right on into the dark.
Those mighty men of timber laid wallowin' in their swallow.
That's why everyone penned the little town "Grog Hollow."
With timber now decreasin', sawmills cease incessant singin';
the glen lies ghostly void of those thousand men a-flingin'.
Laurytown was normal then with just the babblin', bubblin'
      stream
and a handful left remainin' sittin' calmly lost in dream.

Strollin' down the single lane of Laurytown, now Rockport,
I imagine all the sounds of those thousand men of sport.
I sense the trees a-standin' thru a century now or more
are sendin' echo-memories of those good ole' days of yore.

Caring

I returned to the Home of the Shepherd of the Good,
and there with joy, wonder, and compassion so I stood.

    The staff diligently working
        in a dedicated love caring.
    The helped body responding
        in a mutual love sharing.
    The impeded body dedicating
        to fulfilling feats so daring.
    The helpless body reposing
        to understanding love awaring.

We are caring and we are working,
working on the body as a whole,
working on the muscles and on the mind,
working on the bones and on the soul.

We talk and marvel upon the miracles and wonders
      nature performs every day so naturally.
But watch too, all the eyes of helped and helpers,
      determination, thru God's hands-on therapy.

I saw so many joyous wonders
     walking through the halls that day.
Memories now in heart and mind,
     memories that are there to stay.
We cannot thank enough
     these people with their caring hearts,
nor thank God enough,
     being blessed with all our functional body parts.
Yet my mind returns to joyful eyes
     of helped and helper sharing—
all loving, sharing, thru pain unbearing—
     miracles are born from all the loving caring.

We are working and we are caring,
caring for the body as a whole,
caring for the muscles and the mind,
caring for the bones and for the soul.

Valentine's, 1987

I recall a poem written and given
    thirty years ago this day.
One that spoke of growing love
    increasing day by day.

Oftimes the words were silent,
    but the tho'ts were always there.
All I had to say was "I love you,"
    and "Shirl, I do really care."

So on this day called Valentine's,
    accept my deepest love.
And may the years beyond this day
    be as endless as the sky above.

This is your heart night,
    and this is my love.
This is the two of us,
    and to our continual love.

Dreaming

'Tis odd when I'm creative
    and designing many schemes;
poetry takes a back seat;
    good ideas control my dreams.

And, to me, 'tis even odder
    when poetic lines do freeze
that the mind's creative side
    is still functioning with ease.

Should this also be with dreams
    and their creative imagery
when imagination is fertile
    and the mind is moving free?

I know I must be dreaming,
    but my dreams seem locked in sleep.
And for me, at least at present,
    all recall will have to keep.

A Place on Earth

I walk this land softly,
   touching lightly,
      leaving calmly
         all the good things
           upon this good earth.
Take any tree
   that you may see.
From a tiny seed to a towering giant,
   bothering none yet helping all.
      Standing and shading,
      feeding and harboring,
      sheltering and beautifying—
      taking it's place upon this land.
I am a man of this land
   and of this earth.
And if I am to take my place
   as the tree which I now face,
      so be it—so be graced.
I walk this land softly,
   touching lightly,
      leaving calmly
         all the good things
           upon this good earth.
There's a vast bit of difference between
               taking your place
              and taking up space
              on this earth of ours.

Stay by Me

Stay here beside me
    and watch the clouds go dancing by.
    Watch the birds on wing
        and hear them sing
            a melodic lullaby.

Stay here beside me
    and hear me whisper words so tenderly.
    Words of love
        and songs of joy
            to hold in rhythmic harmony.

Stay here beside me
    and help me count all the blessings
        life has given free.
    All the health and love and sons
        we may hold
            in continual reverie.

Stay here beside me
    and hold my hand
        and dance these thoughts with me.
Dance on and on until
        our lives melt
            into spiritual ecstasy.

Stay here beside me
    as we grow and enjoy each passing day,
    until such time
        when we can dance
            the eternal nights away.

Amelia Meets the High Notes

Flair for Poetry

Tho' the mind is holding steady,
my Flair pen stands poised and ready,
     waiting for the thoughts that
     just might break the shell
            where they're confined.

Tho' the words need not be pretty,
nor necessarily too witty,
     'tis the thought that counts
     and just the way the words
            may be assigned.

So, now, isn't it a pity
that this Flair composed no ditty,
     just lines of empty phrases
     with no thoughts of any
            wisdom left behind.

A Rhyme

Apple dapple country squire;
skip around and jump up higher.
Spend the time; go join a choir.
Sing good songs and light your fire.

Drivelling Thoughts

All the dumb drivel that springs from my head
is put down on paper so I know what I've said.
The writings should go to the shredder. Instead,
they end up in someone else's head, I do dread.

A Second Rhyme

Itsy bitsy swizzle stick,
stir the cream, tho' it's so thick.
Why the cow was oh so quick
gives me jitters, makes me sick.

Series of Lonely Thoughts

She's gone.
> Even though for but a little while,
> the heart beats strong;
yet the tho'ts must span the spreaded mile.

►●◄   ►●◄   ►●◄

In her absence,
> I'll compose a poem or so.
Then she'll know
> > I stayed at home
> > and didn't roam
> > all the haunts I know.

►●◄   ►●◄   ►●◄

When she's away,
I hope to play
> all the distaff roles
so common to her day.

►●◄   ►●◄   ►●◄

I do like to be alone,
> if only for a little while.
When she returns to home,
> I'll return it with a happy smile.

►●◄   ►●◄   ►●◄

Lonely are the nights.
Empty are the days.
During the Ides of March,
be sure to mind your ways.

►●◄   ►●◄   ►●◄

Somewhere Out There

Somewhere out there is my land;
  somewhere out there I'll be.
Somewhere out there is my land,
  a land that's clean and free.

When you come out to my land,
  step upon her carefully.
Since all the things on my land
  live in peace and harmony.

To live my life on my land
  that's waiting there for me,
I must be truly ready
  to be accepted gracefully.

D-Day

Dinky dinky dorry due.
Dumbo doggy did do-do.
Dirty deeds did Daddy dread.
Drubbed de dripping doggy dead.

A Third Rhyme

Handsome Harry Sprizzle Spoon.
Could not hold a gosh-darn tune.
Went to school to learn to croon.
Now holds girls in frenzied swoon.

A Fourth Rhyme

Harvey Marvey Bristol Cream.
Start your day beset in dream.
Tho' the tho'ts aren't what they seem,
time will prove they're right on stream.

Time Bandits

I'm taking my time and storing it away.
I'm gonna save it for some cloudy, rainy day.
The only trouble is that when that time is now,
in no time at all, the day is gone somehow.

►•◄   ►•◄   ►•◄

I went to a store to buy some time,
and I ended up just spending it.

►•◄   ►•◄   ►•◄

The best time to get things done
is when there is no time for it.

►•◄   ►•◄   ►•◄

Even if you stick it in a bottle,
the essence of time
cannot be saved, only savored.

►•◄   ►•◄   ►•◄

Take your time;
life is too short if you don't.
And if you don't, I will.
I already have; you've been reading
all this stuff!

►•◄   ►•◄   ►•◄

The Hands of Success

You know,
on the one hand,
in order
to feel safe,
one must have the drive
to push oneself to the limit,
mustering all his strengths
and desires
to the fullest—
all toward a predetermined goal.
He is in conflict
with himself
and with others
in his endeavors
to achieve that goal.
Once that plateau
is achieved,
he is usually satisfied,
unless
his desires and drives
are engulfed with
greed, power, or ambition
to attain an even higher
or different goal.

He remains in the pursuit
                of happiness.

However,
on the other hand,
one who is coming
from the heart
and the mind
and the soul,
sees his safety
in his
inner strengths,
desires,
and energies.
And he is true,
therefore,
to himself.
He is a survivor
of a different kind.
He knows he is at peace
with himself
and with others.
And he knows he is
in harmony
with all of the earth
and the stars
and the creatures of all worlds.
He feels
and sees
and knows
he is what he is.

And he has pursued
         and found happiness.

A Fifth Rhyme

Ragin Cajun Whoopee Snook.
Someone stole my picture book.
When I find that little crook,
he will get one dirty look.

A Sixth Rhyme

Giggle Gargle Gurgle Tease.
Got a cold; excuse me please.
Oh, gee whiz, here comes a sneeze,
handkerchief to nose and squeeze.

A Seventh Rhyme

Horrible Horrible Carson Ditz.
Eats bananas till he loses wits.
Body bulges, then an exploding blitz.
Falls back to earth as banana splits.

A Wandering Soul

When my conscious body is traveling with me,
time becomes the dimension it is meant to be.

> (If my imagination and desires are strong enough, and I have
> a belief in and a knowing of myself, I will be able to wander
> this universe at my leisure and return to my body at my
> pleasure.)

Now time has no dimension and that is also as it is meant to be.

My spirit has a free will, yet is enveloped by my body;
    a temporary keeper am I,
    oh, to let the harbored spirit fly.

> (My earthly mores encourage me to stay firmly on this earth
> and to learn earthly things. I accept that and it is good for
> there is much to learn. Yet my ethereal feelings urge me to
> go forth and become knowing of all these things beyond the
> body and within the soul.
> These nonconflicting mores are really interrelated and the
> growth of one gains wisdom for the other.)

> (Is then the purpose of human life to allow the soul to
> experience all the extensions of wisdom through the
> knowledge gained in the human mind?)

> (Is the mind just a transfer agent to the soul, and the soul a
> prodding questioner into the mind?)

> (If the soul has not gained all the wisdom needed toward
> ultimate ascension, is a return to another body a reincarna-
> tion of the soul?)

There's a wandering soul in my living body now.
　　I'm harboring him and learning all he will allow.
He's asking of me in a gentle prodding way,
　　"Help me to learn from what you've learned today."

If I seek, then surely I shall find
　　the answers to questions within my probing mind.
Then all the knowledge gained will subsequently turn
　　into wisdom for my everlasting soul to learn.

Soul of Mine

Fly with me to the ends of the earth and beyond the azure sky.
Fly until the sky is at the bottom of our feet, and fly on, fly!

Soar until the universe is but a distant glory view.
Soar and soar up, up away 'til we begin our life anew.

Now turn and gather in all the wonders which surround us.
Catch the feeling of all the glorious sights around us.

Reflect on all the good things that happened in our life.
Remember all the happy times which overshadowed those of
    strife.

Keep those memories intact and revered forevermore and longer.
Ne'er forget your friends and loves; the soul grows ever stronger.

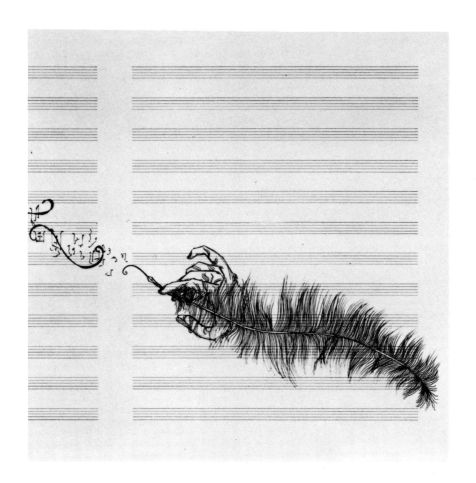

The End

. . . that all those things
your mindsong sings,
the pen in hand will uncover.

—JLH